THE CHINESE
IN AMERICA

THE CHINESE
IN AMERICA

Betty Lee Sung

MACMILLAN PUBLISHING CO., INC.
NEW YORK

COLLIER MACMILLAN PUBLISHERS
LONDON

Macmillan Publishing Co., Inc. 866 Third Avenue, New York, N.Y. 10022
Collier-Macmillan Canada Ltd.
Library of Congress catalog card number: 78-188774
Printed in the United States of America

4 5 6 7 8 9 10

PICTURE CREDITS: American Airlines, 55; California Historical Society, 6;
China Newspicture Service, 85; Columbia University, 102; Culver Pic-
tures, Inc., 33, 40, 51, 54, 68, 72-73, 78; Sen. Hiram Fong, 98; Kenton
Lee, 57; Ellen Levine, 95; Library of Congress, 4, 16-17; Southern
Pacific Railroad, 8, 12, 23; *Today's Health* magazine, 105

CONTENTS

THE CHINESE
IN AMERICA

Chapter One

 ## TO THE MOUNTAIN OF GOLD

The news spread quickly along the wharf in Canton.

"Gold!" they cried. "Gold!"

Fishermen left their sampans. Coolies dropped the baskets suspended from poles on their shoulders. Dock hands stopped in their tracks. Ears perked up. Eyes glistened with excitement and greed.

"Where?" they demanded furiously. "Where? Where?"

"Ask Lao Moy. He heard it from the red-bearded sailor," ventured the coolie Wong.

"Where's Lao Moy?"

"Down by the clipper ship that just weighed anchor."

"You mean the ship is laden with gold?" Everyone was talking at once.

"No, we don't know. Let's go ask Lao Moy."

"You see that crowd? He's over there."

The circle around Lao Moy grew thicker. "Hey, Lao Moy, where's the gold? Did the red-bearded sailor tell you?" the men shouted.

Lao Moy turned at the mention of his name. "Wait, let me start over again. The gold is across the ocean."

The men laughed. It was a joke after all.

Lao Moy continued, "The red-bearded one said the hills are covered with gold. Sometimes with nuggets as big as a hen's egg. No one stops you from taking it if you find it first. The stream beds are lined with gold. And the dirt glistens with gold dust."

"Ahhhh . . ." groaned the crowd. Their eyes gleamed at the prospect.

Then softly, almost in a whisper, Lao Moy said, "The red-bearded one asked me if anybody here wants to go to the Mountain of Gold."

Bursts of laughter greeted this statement. "Some day your sense of humor is going to get you into trouble," warned one of the men. "Across the ocean, indeed! You want us to put our heads on the executioner's chopping block. Better not let the magistrate's soldiers hear you."

Muttering to themselves, the men sauntered back to their tiresome labor. The fishermen picked up their fish to peddle in the streets. The dock hands went back to transporting the piles of wares on the wharves by means of bamboo poles slung across their shoulders thick with calluses. Earning a bare living was bitter, hard labor. To these men, the thought of gold was an unattainable dream. But still, men do dream.

None went with the red-bearded sailor that day. By Chinese tradition, the people seldom roamed far from the ancestral home. But as more and more ships put into port with the same story, the one word —gold—seized the imaginations of a few hardy adventurous souls.

The risks were great. The Mountain of Gold was 7,000 miles across the Pacific Ocean. It was inhabited by white-skinned foreigners who spoke a different tongue and who lived by different customs. Perhaps the red-bearded seaman was lying. Once out of the harbor, the men could be seized and sold into slavery. And if that wasn't enough, the Chinese emperor forbade his subjects to leave the country on pain of death.

These men of southern China came from pioneering stock. Had their forebears not pushed their way southward, expanding the boundaries of the vast domain of China known as the Middle Kingdom?

*Clipper ships brought the first
Chinese immigrants to America*

Now they could push no more. For centuries, they had been stopped by the waters of the Pacific Ocean. But oceans could no longer stop men who dreamed of fortunes in gold.

Furtively and singly, a few bold ones inquired discreetly about passage to the Mountain of Gold. It seemed as if the white men were very anxious to recruit strong, able-bodied men to help work gold claims. Some were smuggled aboard ships to begin the first migration of Chinese to the hills of California. They arrived during the feverish pitch of the Gold Rush in late 1848.

The red-bearded sailor had not lied. The Chinese found gold. The lucky ones picked up large nuggets. Two Chinese found a 240-pound nugget worth over $30,000 at Moore's Flat. A 40-pound nugget was unearthed at the fork of Feather River. But most were content to work the abandoned claims, sift the water and sands of the mountain streams for gold dust, or hire themselves out to men who had discovered rich claims.

News like this spread quickly back to the wharves of Canton, and the rush was on to come to the Mountain of Gold. When the emigrants sent home packets of gold, the emperor relaxed his ban. More and more Chinese left their ancestral home. Within three years, 25,000 Chinese were in California.

The first arrivals found themselves in a new land among very strange people with very strange ways. To ease their fears and sense of loneliness and to find security in the familiar, the Chinese clung together. They spoke their own language, ate their own food, wore the clothes they were accustomed to wearing back home, and followed their own customs and traditions.

*Newcomers from China joined the
search for gold in California*

Of course this attracted a lot of curiosity because the Chinese looked and acted so differently from the white men. For instance, the white men wore coarse clothing with high-laced boots. The Chinese wore loose cotton jackets and trousers and often went barefoot. The white men cut their hair short, but grew beards on their faces. The Chinese were clean shaven, and wore their hair braided in pigtails or queues. They did not like to wear their hair this way, but they had been ordered by the Manchu Emperor to comb their hair in this style. Since they wanted to go back to their homeland, they dared not cut off the queues.

The Chinese, coming from a civilization centuries old, were accustomed to living in an orderly society. They set up organizations on the basis of family or home districts. In this way, the problems of the newcomers were greatly eased. When they were sick, when they needed a place to stay, when they wanted to write a letter home, they knew they could always turn to their family or district association for help.

These associations also acted as employment agencies. Employers who needed extra hands would get in touch with the associations, and men were sent out.

The Chinese had no intention of staying. Few men brought their wives and children with them.

Their goal was to earn enough to buy a little land and set themselves up in business in China. So they worked hard and spent sparingly. The United States was the Mountain of Gold, but China was home.

*Chinese men were
clean shaven and
wore their hair
braided in queues*

Chapter Two

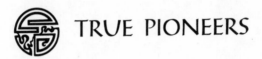 ## TRUE PIONEERS

The scramble for gold was so great that within a very few years most of the surface gold in the hills of California had been taken out. When the abandoned claims yielded less and less, the Chinese turned to other lines of work.

Food was needed to feed the rapidly growing population of California. To bring in food and supplies from the East or across the Pacific was both costly and uncertain. The California climate was mild and ideal for agricultural purposes. But most of the swashbuckling pioneers who had trekked thousands of miles across a continent were looking for a quick bonanza. They were not interested in growing crops.

So the tomatoes burst their fiery red jackets, and overripe fruits fell to the ground to rot, because there were no hands to bring in the crops.

The farmers went to the Chinese associations and contracted for hired workers to plow the fields, cultivate the crops, and bring in the harvest. At the break of day every morning, the contracted workers would appear at the farms, do their work efficiently and quietly, and slip away at sundown.

News like this traveled quickly, so that by 1884, half of the farm workers in California were Chinese. These men came from a long line of farmers who knew how to coax the most from the earth or starve. No wonder they made such good farmers.

Much of the city of San Francisco today stands on man-made land. When the first white settlers saw her, she was a half-submerged peninsula of marshes and swamps. Needless to say, there were no drainage machinery, bulldozers, or trucks in those days. Malaria took a heavy toll of white laborers who tried to fill in the land. Once more the work fell to the hardy Chinese who reclaimed more than five million acres of lush garden and farm land at the mouths of the San Joaquin and Sacramento Rivers.

Skilled Chinese labor also gave impetus to the budding industries of the West, so that these goods did not have to be shipped all the way from the East Coast. The shoe industry is a good example.

*In 1864 many Chinese
in America were hired
as construction workers
to build the first
transcontinental railroad*

In 1864, the Chinese went into an entirely new line of work—railroad construction.

At that time, a journey from the East to the West was long and hazardous. There were three choices of travel. One was to sail around the tip of South America, a dangerous trip on the high seas that took approximately three months. The second was to take the land route across the American continent over the Rocky Mountains, across the burning deserts, through hostile Indian territory, and across the crags of the Sierra Nevadas. The hazards of these cross-country covered-wagon treks are well-known sagas of western lore.

The third choice was to take a ship down to the Isthmus of Panama, get off, cross the swamps of that narrow landstrip by foot, where malaria and yellow fever took many victims, and wait, perhaps months, for another ship to sail up the West Coast.

Such poor transportation and communications isolated the West from the East and kept the country divided.

To weld this nation into one, and to prevent the western frontier from coming under Mexican, British, or Russian spheres of influence, Congress authorized the building of a transcontinental railroad. The Union Pacific and the Central Pacific were commissioned to do the job.

The Union Pacific was to start at the Missouri

River and build westward, while the Central Pacific was to begin from the West Coast and build eastward. Both rails were to link up and form one continuous line upon completion.

An immediate cry went up for men, for boys, for any pair of hands that could do the work. But at that time, the country was embroiled in the Civil War. Manpower was not to be had. Of the thousands hired in 1863 and 1864 and sent into the hills, only two out of five reported for work. Most of the time, the Central Pacific had less than 600 men on its work force.

At that rate, it seemed as if the railroad would never be built until someone suggested using the Chinese. "What?" protested the superintendent of labor, J. H. Strobridge. "Those puny Chinamen! They're not capable of doing such heavy manual labor."

Dubiously, however, he agreed to try the experiment. Fifty Chinese were hired and given picks, shovels, and wheelbarrows. All through the day, the engineers expected the "weaklings" to fall in their tracks, but at the end of a twelve-hour day, the engineers were pleased and astonished with the results. Their opinion of the Chinese quickly changed.

Like everything else that they applied themselves to, the Chinese became adept at building railroads. At one time, over 10,000 Chinese worked for the

Central Pacific. Some of the men were hired locally through the associations. Others were recruited under contract from China. Their heroism in building the transcontinental railroad, undoubtedly the greatest engineering feat of the nineteenth century, is described vividly in the book *The Big Four*, by Oscar Lewis.

According to Lewis, the most dangerous work was the drilling and placing of explosives that literally blasted out a narrow ledge along the granite walls of the Sierra Nevadas. Swarming over the upper canyons, the men pecked away at the broken rocks of the cuts with their picks. Trooping in long lines beneath their basket hats, they poured wheelbarrow-loads of debris down the canyon side. Their nimble feet trod precariously along the ledges, carrying seventy-pound kegs of black powder suspended from both ends of bamboo poles. Wrote Lewis:

> Cape Horn, a sheer granite buttress, proved the most formidable obstacle of the year; its lower sides dropped away in a thousand-foot vertical cliff that offered no vestige of a foothold. The indomitable Chinese were lowered from above on ropes, and there suspended between sky and earth, chipped away with hammer and chisel to form the first precarious ledge which was then laboriously deepened to a shelf wide enough to permit the passage of cars

Chinese laborers built the timber railroad trestles bridging many of the High Sierra chasms

In testimony before Congress, Oswald Garrison Villard paid tribute to the heroism of the Chinese workers on the railroads. He said:

> I want to remind you of the things that Chinese labor did for us in opening up the western portion of this country. I am a son of the man who drove the first transcontinental railroad across the American Northwest, the first rail link from Minnesota to Oregon and the waters of the Puget Sound. I was near him when he drove the last spike and paid an eloquent tribute to the men who had built that railroad by their manual labor for there were no road-making machines in those days.
>
> He never forgot and never failed to praise the Chinese, of whom nearly 10,000 stormed the forest fastnesses, endured cold and heat and the risk of death at the hands of the hostile Indians to aid in the opening up of our great northwestern empire.
>
> I have a dispatch from the chief engineer of the Northwestern Pacific telling how the Chinese laborers went out into eight feet of snow with the temperature far below zero to carry on the work when no American dared face the conditions.

Early historians agree that the contributions made by the pioneer Chinese to the opening up and the rapid development of the West are great.

Wherever the Chinese went, they were welcomed

and praised for their hard work, their reliability, their honor, and their orderliness. Whatever they did, they did well. In 1852, Governor McDougal of California recommended a system of land grants to induce the further immigration and settlement of the Chinese whom he called "one of the most worthy of our newly adopted citizens."

Chapter Three

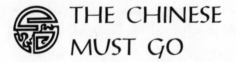 THE CHINESE
MUST GO

On May 10, 1869, at 2:47 P.M. Eastern time, W. N. Shilling, telegraph operator, put his finger to the telegraph key. He tapped out three dots. This was the signal to waiting crowds across the nation.

In Washington, D.C., a magnetic ball fell from the dome of the Capitol building. A roar rose from the crowds gathered on the Capitol steps. At the same moment in San Francisco, the city went wild. Fire bells pealed from the City Hall tower. The boom of 220 guns from Fort Point split the air. In Philadelphia, the Liberty Bell chimed. Throughout the nation, the people were celebrating a historic moment taking place on Promontory Point, Utah.

The last tie had been laid in place. The last spike, forged of gold, had been hammered in. The tracks of the Central Pacific and Union Pacific were one. The transcontinental railroad was completed. The nation was now joined.

Bret Harte, editor of the San Francisco *Overland Monthly*, seized his pen and scribbled a poem:

> What was it the engines said,
> Pilots touching, head to head,
> Facing on a single track,
> Half a world behind each back?

The transcontinental railroad had been scheduled for completion in fourteen years. In the beginning, scarcity of labor threatened to drag things out. But in half the time, seven years, to be exact, the task was done. To the young American nation, proud of its monumental feat, the railroad seemingly offered boundless horizons. While the country went wild with joy, 25,000 men who had worked on the railroad found themselves out of jobs.

Now that it was easy to ride the rails, thousands streamed west. When they got there, they found that the Gold Rush was over. The catch phrase, "Go west, young man, go west," rang hollow. There were lots of men competing for the same jobs.

The West was frontier country and growing so fast that the laws could not keep up with the changes. Disputes were settled with guns. Historian H. H. Bancroft claimed that there were more than four saloons for every street corner in San Francisco. Drunken brawls, murder, and crime were commonplace.

When the market fell through in the Comstock Lode mining stocks in 1876, a depression set in. Everyone was hard hit. Discontent and grumbling became widespread. A scapegoat was needed, and the Chinese were the most obvious.

With their long queues, foreign dress, clannish ways, and docile manner, the Chinese were a perfect target. They had jobs. The white men did not. It didn't matter that the white men scorned the jobs that the Chinese held. The white man was looking to get rich quick, whereas the Chinese were willing to work long, hard hours.

So where the Chinese had once been praised for their hard work, their honesty, their thrift, and peaceful ways, they were now charged with being coolies, dangerous and deceitful. They were accused of working for slave wages and undermining the white man's standard of living.

During this period, they were stoned, robbed, beaten, and massacred. Special taxes were levied, which were paid almost entirely by the Chinese. Severe laws were passed against them. Employers no longer dared hire them. They were driven from their camps and their quarters burned.

The Chinese were helpless. Neither the police, the state, nor the federal government gave them protection.

They had no legal recourse because a judge ruled that their word could not be accepted in court.

They could not farm because they were not permitted to own land.

They could not get jobs because they were not permitted to join the unions.

The foreign dress and unfamiliar customs of the Chinese often made them targets of discrimination

They could not apply for citizenship for the silly reason that they were neither white nor black.

They were restricted to living in Chinatowns, where they lived in constant fear for their lives and property. Attacks against the Chinese became so wanton and outrageous that decent citizens formed vigilante groups to protect these hapless souls.

It was hard to believe that the attitude toward the Chinese could be so drastically reversed. Even Leland Stanford, one of the Big Four partners for whom the Chinese built the Central Pacific, made a complete about-face. Once he had praised them. When he ran for public office in California for governor and senator, he found it to his advantage politically to condemn them.

Harsh measures were not enough. In their frenzied prejudice, the Californians wanted to get rid of all the Chinese. The cry rose to an insistent demand. The Chinese must go!

On the other side of the Pacific Ocean, China was just coming into contact with Western civilization. For centuries, China had been the center of the Eastern Hemisphere. At one time, her empire spread from the northernmost tip of Korea to the South China Sea. From east to west, the area was equally vast—from Taiwan to Asia Minor.

These countries paid tribute to the emperor in Peking. The influence of Chinese civilization—her arts, her literature, her culture, her thoughts—reached into all these regions. China was a proud nation. She had no need for the Western nations that came knocking at her door.

American merchants were clamoring to get into China. With their new fleet of clipper ships they found that their cargoes of silk, tea, porcelains, ivories, and works of art from the East brought them huge profits in Boston and New York. They wanted to get into China to trade. But the emperor said no. The white man was not welcome.

In 1860, the American government sent a diplomat by the name of Anson Burlingame to pry open the doors of China. For six years he stayed in Peking, slowly winning the friendship and confidence of the Imperial Court. Finally he negotiated a treaty that guaranteed to the citizens of both countries the right to live and travel in the other's country.

The treaty also pledged that the emperor would protect all American citizens within Chinese borders and that the American government would do the same for all Chinese subjects.

The Burlingame Treaty was hailed by the president and the United States Senate as a triumph in American diplomacy. China had opened her doors. American traders could now go in.

The Burlingame Treaty was ratified in 1868. The

transcontinental railroad was completed in 1869. Shortly thereafter anti-Chinese feelings set in.

The American government conveniently ignored its treaty obligations. It gave the Chinese no protection against the wrath of the West. At the same time, it insisted upon its treaty rights for its citizens in China.

In 1882, in direct contravention of the treaty, Congress passed the first of the infamous Chinese exclusion acts, which suspended Chinese immigration for ten years.

Regularly thereafter, whenever an election came up, the Chinese question would be thrown into the political arena. The candidates would call for harsher laws and an extension of the period banning the Chinese from American shores. It didn't matter that Chinese immigration had been reduced to a few students, teachers, merchants, officials, and travelers. The issue was a good political football.

For example, in the year just before the first exclusion act was passed in 1882, 40,000 Chinese entered the United States. In 1887, only ten were admitted. But an election was coming up, so the politicians made a big campaign issue out of an almost nonexistent problem.

They passed the Scott Act, which prohibited Chinese laborers from entering the United States. Even those who had left the country for temporary visits and who held re-entry permits were not allowed to return. About 20,000 Chinese who may have had families, businesses, and property here were shut out in this highhanded fashion.

Four years passed. Things quieted down for a while until another election fanned the flames of anti-Chinese feelings. This time, Congress passed the Geary Act of 1892. The act extended all bills in force against the Chinese for another ten years. It practically stripped the Chinese of any protection in court. Every Chinese in the United States had to get a certificate of eligibility to remain in the country.

In 1898, when Hawaii was annexed to the United States, Congress made all the anti-Chinese laws applicable to that territory in spite of the fact that Chinese immigration had never been an issue in Hawaii, and the Chinese there were well assimilated.

The same thing happened in the Philippines when those islands came under American rule, although for centuries Filipino-Chinese relations had been warm and friendly. Altogether fourteen laws relating to Chinese exclusion were passed, each one more severe than the one before.

Even American-born Chinese, with every right as United States citizens, were harassed and detained if they made a trip to China. They were never permitted to step from ship to shore, but were locked up in Ellis Island or Angel's Island—sometimes for weeks or months—where they were questioned or grilled about their right to enter the country.

No matter how long a Chinese lived in the United States, he was not permitted to apply for citizenship. Up until the Civil War, only free white men were allowed to become naturalized citizens. The Fourteenth and Fifteenth Amendments to the Constitution extended this right to the black man. Since they were neither black nor white, the courts ruled that the Chinese were "aliens ineligible for citizenship."

Never in the history of the United States had the nationals of another friendly sovereign nation been so humiliated, so disgraced, so persecuted. The Chinese were the only people specifically named by law to be barred from the country. The phrase "not a Chinaman's chance" was born of this period and came to mean no chance whatsoever. It accurately reflected the position of the Chinese at that time.

Chapter Four

 LAUNDRYMEN

In China, most of the people earned their living by farming. Some who lived near rivers and the ocean were fishermen. Others were peddlers or craftsmen.

Land was very scarce, and the large number of people dependent upon it made matters worse. The land was intensely cultivated. Every nook and corner was used to grow food. Even the mountains were terraced, and crops were planted as high as the weather permitted. In the colder regions of the mountaintops, tea was grown.

In spite of these intense efforts, the land did not yield enough to feed the people. Life was hard and the people were poor.

The dream of fortunes in gold lured the Chinese across 7,000 miles of ocean to a foreign land. But what started out as a dream became a nightmare.

History is best seen through the experiences of the people who lived it. Tin Fook's story is typical of what the Chinese went through in the early days of the development of the West.

Tin Fook pressed his face against the cracks in the floorboards. His eyes were round with fear. Above him, the scuffling of heavy boots scraped back and forth accompanied by crashing thuds as the band of marauders pulled things from the shelves and over-turned the wooden chests.

His heart sank when he saw that the men had uncovered his father's little hoard of gold. He almost cried out in rage when the men pocketed it and left the little cabin in complete disorder. But Tin Fook had been warned by his father to hide beneath the boards and to keep still whenever the drunken white men came to plunder.

When the men had gone, Tin Fook sobbed until he was exhausted. He longed for his mother and grandmother in China. He missed his little sister dreadfully. At twelve years of age, he was still a boy, but in many respects he was doing a grown man's job.

Tin Fook had come to this strange land known as the Mountain of Gold with his father, his elder cousin, and his uncles after one of their trips home to China. The men had spoken glowingly of their adventures in the land beyond the Pacific Ocean. Tin Fook had listened with rapt attention to stories of their ocean voyage, their search for gold, and their tales about men from all corners of the globe. He had wanted to come with his father and uncles, although they had had a hard time persuading his mother to let him go.

Now that he was 7,000 miles away from home, he was homesick, heartsick, and afraid. Every morning, Tin Fook's father and uncles went to work—sometimes on farms, sometimes in drainage work, and sometimes on construction jobs.

When employers needed workers, they contacted the associations in Chinatown. These served as agencies for recruiting Chinese labor. There were always calls for men, and the Chinese were seldom idle.

Tin Fook was too young for the heavy work that the men did. He stayed home and took care of the cabin where they lived in an abandoned mining camp.

More than twenty years had passed since gold was discovered on the American River nearby, and most of the gold had been taken out. The cabins were now inhabited mainly by colonies of Chinese laborers.

When Tin Fook's father and uncles came home

that night, they shrugged their shoulders. "We are helpless," they sighed. "The white men have turned against us. They come in to rob us, beat us, and kill us whenever they get drunk. If we resist, they go away and come back with more men. Public officials not only give us no protection, they even stir up trouble."

"Let's go home," begged Tin Fook. "Let's go home. I do not like these bad men."

"We will, my son," soothed Father. "As soon as we save up a little more money we will go home."

"How are we ever going to save anything if we get robbed every time we manage to put away a little gold?" ventured Elder Cousin.

"You are right," Uncle put in. "Every day the rowdies make it more difficult for us to find work. Why don't we leave now with our health and our lives? We can go inland. I hear it is not as bad in the East."

So it was that those who had saved enough went back to China. Those who wanted to make a little more began to leave California and disperse eastward. But the anti-Chinese campaign had succeeded in whipping up a frenzied hatred of the Chinese everywhere.

Employers who may have preferred hiring Chinese were intimidated or prevented from doing so. The Chinese would have liked to farm, but many states passed Alien Land Acts that forbade them to own land. The unions kept them out of organized trades and factories. Persecuted and harassed, the Chinese were forced to look for other means of livelihood.

They soon found out that the scarcity of women in the frontier lands meant that duties like washing and ironing and cooking went begging at high wages. Many Chinese took jobs as houseboys, servants, and cooks. Others went into business for themselves by opening laundries and restaurants. No matter where the Chinese went, opening a laundry was a fairly simple matter. A scrub board, an iron and ironing board, a small place, and one was in business.

A contemporary drawing showed Chinese laundrymen washing clothes on rafts in the river

Most laundries were one- or two-man shops. Each laundry took in only as much as it could handle. Expenses and rent were low. Little knowledge of the English language was necessary.

In this type of self-employment, the Chinese did not have to compete with the white man on an unequal basis. He did not have to go and ask the white man for a job. He was not afraid of being fired or laid off first because his skin was yellow.

The laundryman was his own boss. If he worked hard, he earned enough to support himself and sometimes many family members in China who depended upon him. He was self-sufficient.

Somehow, the white man did not mind the Chinese doing this type of "woman's work." So they left him alone. From dawn to dusk the laundryman scrubbed and washed and toiled over a hot iron. If it was a one-man shop, he seldom had anyone to talk to in his own language from Sunday to Sunday.

He saw his work as a lowly, menial job, which he endured because other types of work were closed to him. Nevertheless he kept at it because he had a purpose and a goal. That was to save enough so that he could go back to China. There he could buy a little land or go into business, build a house, and send his children to school. Life held little promise for him here, where he could not become a citizen and could not participate in American life. His only dream lay across the Pacific Ocean.

So the American people came to know the Chinese mainly as a laundryman with his bundles of clean white clothes. Some find it hard to think of the Chinese as anything else. This popular image persists in spite of the fact that fewer and fewer Chinese now enter this line of work.

When the barriers of prejudice were let down after World War II, the Chinese turned to the professions in increasing numbers. Almost one out of five Chinese in this country works as an engineer, doctor, scientist, or teacher. Only the old immigrants and a few newcomers still operate laundries.

Chapter Five

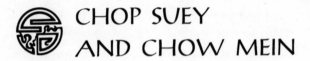 CHOP SUEY
AND CHOW MEIN

In the Gold Rush days of California, there were many eating places that served Chinese food. The Chinese were not accustomed to Western food. They preferred what they were used to. What was surprising, though, was how popular this food became with non-Chinese people.

Late one night at a small place operated by two brothers, a group of hungry miners banged on the door.

"Open up," roared the miners. "Open up, or we will break the door down."

With each thump, the door hinges creaked and groaned.

Behind the door, Kun Sing crouched in fright. "What will we do, Elder Brother? We are all sold out, and we have no food left."

"If we don't let them in, they'll break the door down. And if we don't give them something to eat, they'll tear the place apart. Open the door first, and I'll think of something," replied Kun Hing as he scurried about the kitchen.

When the doors were unlocked, six hungry miners tramped in. "We want something to eat," they demanded. "Bring us some food."

Kun Sing backed away toward the kitchen. "Please wait a little while," he pleaded. He knew these men. They were coarse and rough and bad-tempered, especially when they had been drinking. They must have had quite a few drinks, since it was late Saturday night.

In the kitchen, Kun Hing had found some celery and onions. He poked around and came up with some *bok-toy*, a Chinese cabbage. A few bamboo shoots were lying around. "Look and see if you can find some scraps of meat," he directed Kun Sing. There was some leftover rice. With these ingredients, he concocted a large platterful, which he set before the miners.

The miners attacked the food with gusto. It was devoured in no time. "Hey, this is good chow," exclaimed the miners. "What do you call this dish?"

Kun Sing looked at his brother. On the spur of the moment, Kun Hing replied, "Chop suey," meaning a miscellaneous mixture. From that day on, whenever the miners came in, they would ask for chop suey and nothing else. Soon the other miners began asking for chop suey at other eating places. Chop suey as a favorite Chinese food was established.

Another version of how chop suey began goes like this: In 1896, Li Hung Chang, viceroy and foreign minister of China, made a good-will tour to Russia. He decided to go back to China by way of England and the United States. When he sailed into New York harbor, he was greeted by a nineteen-gun salute. The Sixth Cavalry escorted him from the dock to the Waldorf Astoria Hotel for his five-day state visit.

On the second day, President Cleveland came to pay his respects. He was accompanied by the leading statesmen of the nation.

The kitchen and chefs of the world-famous Waldorf Astoria were ready to serve Li the best in food and drink. He was invited to feasts and banquets, but Li would eat only the food prepared by his own chefs. When asked what he was eating, Li replied, "Chop suey." He invited his hosts to taste it. A few mouthfuls convinced them. Newspapers spread the story, and chop suey became popular.

Chow mein, another supposedly Chinese dish, also originated in the United States. Chow mein means fried noodles. Some kind of meat or shrimp, bean sprouts, celery, and onions are cooked together and served over a generous portion of crisp, deep-fried noodles. The noodles give the dish its crunchy flavor.

According to legend, a chef once dropped some noodles into a pot of deep fat by mistake. The noodles turned crisp and golden brown. The thrifty chef did not want to throw away the noodles so he served them to his customers anyway. They thought the meal was delicious and that is how chow mein got started.

Chop suey and chow mein became the mainstays of Chinese restaurants and gave impetus to the second most important occupation of the Chinese in America.

Like laundries, cooking in the Western frontier was considered woman's work. The men did not want to do it. But they did enjoy good food. If they had labored a whole week out in the hills, they liked to come to town on weekends and get some solid meals under their belts.

On their part, the Chinese were particularly suited by temperament and tradition to operate restaurants. The pleasures of cooking and the enjoyment of eating are an important part of Chinese cul-

ture way back into history. Chinese writers and poets sang of food as Western poets sang of love.

The Chinese cuisine is considered one of the best in the world. Down through the centuries, the Chinese have learned how to combine ingredients and spices and flavors. Experience taught them to eat a large variety of foods. Texture, cooking time, and even the way the food is sliced or cut are all important factors. The amount of time and attention devoted to the preparation of food is great, so that cooking in China is considered an art—not a chore.

Circumstances edged the Chinese into this line of work. Chinese restaurants soon dotted the American scene. Chop suey and chow mein became popular restaurant fare. Once again, the Chinese proved that they could accommodate themselves to a situation that gave them little choice.

This market offered
a wide assortment
of the varied ingredients
used in Chinese cuisine

Chapter Six

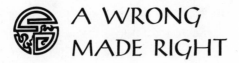 A WRONG
MADE RIGHT

The number of Chinese in the United States dwindled. Few came in. Others left. They scattered. By 1940 there were only about 78,000 Chinese in all of the United States.

Then came Pearl Harbor. The Japanese bombed the American fleet in Hawaii. War was declared. The United States found itself an ally of China, which had been fighting alone against the Japanese since 1937. At that point the laws discriminating against the Chinese in America became a source of embarrassment to the government.

Accordingly, President Franklin D. Roosevelt called for repeal of the exclusion acts by saying,

"Nations, like individuals, make mistakes. We must be big enough to acknowledge our mistakes of the past and to correct them."

Congress agreed. The exclusion laws were repealed in 1943. Chinese living in the United States were finally granted the right to apply for citizenship. China was given a quota, which permitted 105 persons to enter the country each year.

This was such a tiny quota that it was almost the same as exclusion. At the rate of 105 a year, the list of applicants stretched way into the twenty-first century. In comparison, Great Britain had an annual quota of 65,361; Germany, 25,814. Even a very small country like the Netherlands had 3,136.

The tiny quota caused the Chinese untold heartaches. Most of the Chinese in America were middle-aged men whose wives and children were in China. Since their families were not allowed to enter the country, it was their custom to go back to China every so often for a visit.

World War II kept the families apart until 1946. When peace came, the men rushed back to China to see their wives and children. Three years later, the Communists had taken over the mainland, and the men were again cut off from their loved ones. They could not go back to China to see their families, nor could they bring them to the United States.

For most, the quota of 105 meant that they would

be tottering with old age or dead and gone long before their turn came around. They were condemned to a life of loneliness and separation from their families because of a law that continued the policy of discrimination against the Chinese.

Gradually Congress loosened the restrictions. First they allowed the men who had acquired United States citizenship to send for their wives and children. Then on several occasions special legislation was passed permitting a few thousand refugees to enter.

The numbers were never large, and the quota of 105 remained in effect for almost a quarter of a century.

In 1965, sweeping changes were made in the archaic United States immigration laws. The rule of admitting immigrants on the basis of country of origin or by race was abolished. First come, first served was the new yardstick. Preference was given to family members and applicants with needed skills.

The new law did not go into effect until 1968. So it is only recently that the Chinese have been permitted to enter the country to any extent, to become citizens, or even to begin to live normal family lives.

Consequently, the Chinese population in the United States is a rather small one. Over the span of a century, from 1860 to 1960, the number of Chinese on the mainland United States was never more than 200,000. When Hawaii was included in the

Chinese Population by States
1970

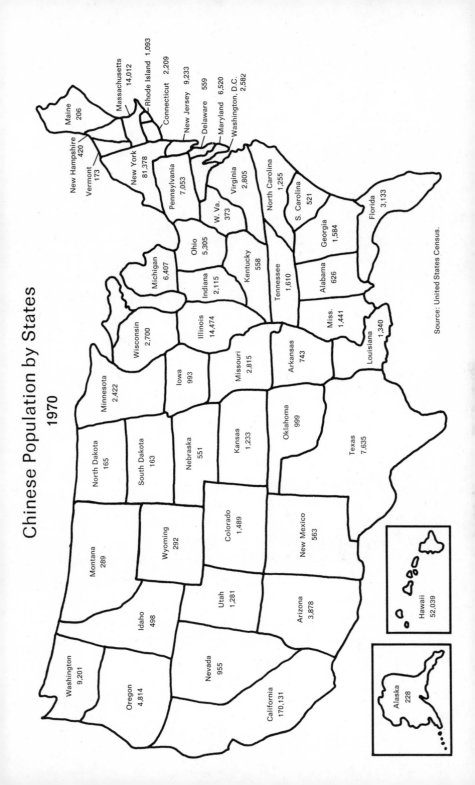

Source: United States Census.

Washington 9,201
Oregon 4,814
California 170,131
Nevada 955
Idaho 498
Utah 1,281
Arizona 3,878
Montana 289
Wyoming 292
Colorado 1,489
New Mexico 563
North Dakota 165
South Dakota 163
Nebraska 551
Kansas 1,233
Oklahoma 999
Texas 7,635
Minnesota 2,422
Iowa 993
Missouri 2,815
Arkansas 743
Louisiana 1,340
Wisconsin 2,700
Illinois 14,474
Michigan 6,407
Indiana 2,115
Ohio 5,305
Kentucky 558
Tennessee 1,610
Miss. 1,441
Alabama 626
Georgia 1,584
Florida 3,133
S. Carolina 521
North Carolina 1,255
Virginia 2,805
W. Va. 373
Pennsylvania 7,053
New York 81,378
Maine 206
New Hampshire 420
Vermont 173
Massachusetts 14,012
Rhode Island 1,093
Connecticut 2,209
New Jersey 9,233
Delaware 559
Maryland 6,520
Washington, D.C. 2,582
Hawaii 52,039
Alaska 228

CHINESE POPULATION IN THE UNITED STATES
1860 to 1970

Year	Number
1970	435,062
1960	237,292
1950	117,629
1940	77,504
1930	74,954
1920	61,639
1910	71,531
1900	89,863
1890	107,488
1880	105,465
1870	63,199
1860	34,933

Source: United States Census

census count of 1960, the total came to 237,000. However, the 1970 census showed that the Chinese-American population had doubled in ten years to 435,000. Yet this number is very, very small in relation to total United States population and in comparison with other national groups.

There are Americans of Chinese descent living in every state of the Union, but two out of three live in just three states: California, New York, and Hawaii.

California has almost 40 per cent of the Chinese population in this country. New York has 18 per cent, and Hawaii 11 per cent. The rest are scattered throughout the other forty-seven states. There are even 228 in Alaska.

Hawaii did not become a state until 1959. But its history of Chinese immigration goes back to the days of the 1850s, when the sugar plantation owners needed men to work the fields. Many Chinese went to Hawaii where they were welcomed and well liked. When those islands were annexed as an American territory in 1898, the Chinese exclusion laws were extended to Hawaii, and further immigration was cut off. Before American annexation, one out of every five persons in Hawaii was of Chinese descent. The rate today is roughly one out of every sixteen.

Not only are the Chinese concentrated in three states, they live primarily in only a few of the large western and eastern cities. These are San Francisco, Honolulu, New York, and Los Angeles. This concentration makes it seem as if there are more Chinese than the actual count.

A very peculiar aspect of the Chinese-American population for many years was that it consisted almost totally of full-grown men. There were few women and children. Among the reasons were:

Chinese family bonds were very strong. Few people left the ancestral home for long. If the men had to leave to earn a livelihood, they left their wives and children at home.

The ocean voyage from southern China to a wild frontierland was dangerous. Only strong, able-bodied men ventured to make the journey.

The enactment of the exclusion laws dating from 1882 made it impossible for the women and children to join their menfolk even if they wanted to do so later on.

In 1900, the census revealed that there were nineteen Chinese males to every Chinese female in the United States. This lopsided situation has been corrected to a large extent because most of the recent immigrants have been wives and children reunited with their husbands and fathers.

When the Chinese were excluded from the United States and not allowed to become citizens, the few who remained worked hard and spent little. The money they earned they sent to China for the support of their families. When they had saved up a little sum, they invariably left the country. Life here was just a temporary stay.

But the picture has changed. The immigration laws are more equitable. The Chinese can pledge allegiance to the United States by becoming citizens. Incidents of discrimination are isolated. With the major barriers removed, the Chinese have done well economically and socially.

Now that the families are reunited in this country, the Chinese prefer to stay and call this land home.

Chapter Seven

 CHINATOWNS

In the shadow of City Hall, not far from the tip of Manhattan Island, there are a number of blocks unlike any other in New York City. The streets are narrow and winding, laid out over a hundred years ago. Most of the buildings are just as old, but some of the more recent structures are capped with red-tiled roofs and gilded eaves that curve skyward.

Balconies, typical of Chinese architecture, run across the façade of the upper stories. The Oriental imprint is seen in the street signs, the public telephone booths, the neon lights, and even the memorial arch dedicated to men who died in the armed services of the United States.

The narrow streets are filled to overflowing with people chattering away in their own tongue. Most of them are speaking Toishanese or Cantonese, dialects commonly spoken in a southern province of China. Sometimes Mandarin, the northern dialect, is heard too.

The windows of food stores are filled with vegetables and groceries not found in the ordinary supermarket. There are lotus roots, fresh ginger, winter melons, victory gourds, bean sprouts, bamboo shoots, water chestnuts, bean curd, taro roots, hairy melons, snow peas, and many other vegetables that are not native to this country. Sugar-cured ducks and whole roast pigs hang from hooks in the stores. They do not hang there for long because they are bought very quickly. Other unusual foods are sea slugs and thousand-year eggs. These eggs are not really a thousand years old; they may be only three months old. Centuries ago, the Chinese found a way to preserve eggs other than by drying or salting them. The eggs are buried in mud mixed with calcium. They age and turn black but do not spoil. They have a very special flavor and are considered a delicious delicacy.

Over two hundred restaurants are found within these few city blocks. These restaurants not only cater to the Chinese, but also to a vast number of non-Chinese people who come to enjoy such dishes

Markets in Chinatown are filled with vegetables and groceries not found in ordinary supermarkets

as shark's fin soup, five-flavored duck, snow peas with diced lobster, butterfly shrimp and hundreds of other strange-sounding foods.

Teahouses serve *dim sum*, little bite-size pastries made of paper-thin rice dough with sweet or meat fillings. The customer has a choice of black teas, red teas, green teas, or teas flavored with flower petals.

The curio shops are filled with art objects from the Orient. There may be tall porcelain vases, long rice-paper scrolls, teakwood furniture inlaid with mother-of-pearl, carved ivory figures, precious jade ornaments, big brass gongs, and many other works of art. The Chinese love beauty. Their artistic nature found expression in many, many forms—in paintings, in intricate carvings, in sculpture, in embroideries, in weaving, and so on.

Thousands of years ago, the Chinese learned how to make porcelain. They mixed clay with bone, molded it into utensils, and baked them in a very hot oven. Gradually they added designs and glazes to their porcelains to make them beautiful. When samples of these dishes, bowls, and vases were brought to the West, porcelain became known as china.

Every day, thousands of tourists come to this section of the city called Chinatown. They come by car and by subway. Sometimes they come in busloads. They come to sightsee, to shop, and to dine in the restaurants. They are fascinated by what they see because to them, everything is unusual. A trip to Chinatown is exciting, but few tourists go away with any knowledge of how Chinatowns came about. Nor do they learn much about the people, the customs, and the culture of the community.

Chinatowns are found in many large American cities. The oldest and the largest one is in San Francisco. Other well-known Chinatowns are in Los Angeles, Sacramento, Chicago, Boston, and Philadelphia as well as the one in New York City.

When the Chinese first came to this country, they found themselves in a strange land among strange people, who spoke different languages and practiced different customs. It was natural for the Chinese to want to live together in one area, so that they would feel more comfortable and could follow their own ways.

In living together, the early Chinese found strength and security. Following the strong family tradition in China, the Chinese organized themselves in associations based on family name. There are only 438 family names for the seven hundred million Chinese throughout the world. Some of the most common ones are Wong, Chin, Moy, Lee, and Woo. Millions of Chinese have the surname Wong. All these Wongs think of themselves as belonging to the Wong family.

*The oldest and largest
Chinatown in the
United States is
in San Francisco*

The colorful streets of
Los Angeles's Chinatown
are lined with
pagoda-roofed buildings

Those without family connections sought ties with others coming from the same home district in China. Most of the Chinese in the United States come from a region in southern China in and around the city of Canton.

The associations served as centers where their members could go to seek help when in need, to find jobs, and to settle disputes. When employers needed workers, they knew they could arrange through the associations to hire a certain number of men.

In the event of death, the associations arranged to have the bones of the deceased sent back to the ancestral village. The Chinese did not want their souls wandering around in a foreign land.

Chinatown governed itself through these organizations. Disputes were settled by family elders. Group pressure was enough to make the members abide by the rulings. The Chinese seldom took their problems to governmental agencies or to the courts, for the simple fact was their word was not accepted as testimony.

During the period of intense persecution, the Chinese sought protection within the boundaries of Chinatown. Later on, private agreements called "restrictive covenants" prevented the Chinese from living elsewhere. So it was that both from choice and on account of discrimination, the Chinese established Chinatowns wherever they went. And in their

*Many Chinese-American children learn
to read and write Chinese characters*

Chinatowns, they devised ways to meet their own wants and their own needs.

One of their intense desires was to preserve their culture and heritage. It is a proud heritage that goes back more than four thousand years. Chinese schools in Chinatown teach the language, the history, and the thoughts of China's great men. Many Chinese-American children attend public school from nine in the morning until three in the afternoon. Then they go to Chinese school for another two hours every day.

The Chinese language is written in characters from top to bottom and from right to left. Each character, which appears somewhat square in shape, is one syllable. Chinese is a picture language. To learn how to read and write, the student must memorize thousands of characters and expressions. He does not have an alphabet to help him with the pronunciation or spelling.

An example of how the Chinese used to solve their banking problem is seen in their credit clubs. The reluctance of American banks to loan them money made it difficult for most Chinese to obtain funds for business purposes or for emergency needs. So they formed credit clubs through the family associations. Members who wanted to save money would bring it to their family association, and the funds were loaned out to other members. Naturally the borrowers paid interest for the use of the money. Such credit clubs are no longer necessary. Today, many modern banks have branches in Chinatowns, with Chinese-speaking personnel.

The Chinese do not believe there is only one God. They think that all religions teach men to be good. For centuries, they lived according to the teachings of Confucius, Lao Tze, and Buddha. But since the first arrival of Chinese immigrants in this country, the Christian missions have played an important role in Chinatown. That is why the religious life of the community centers more around Christian churches than Buddhist or Confucian temples. There are many Christian churches in Chinatown and they provide valuable services to the people. These include English classes, recreational facilities, and of course religious guidance. Some of the earlier missions even provided medical care.

For thousands of years, the Chinese cured their sick with skills and medicinal herbs handed down from generation to generation. From experience, they learned that a certain bark, a certain root, a certain plant will reduce fever, build up the blood, or clear away an infection. Although few studies have been made of this branch of medicine to determine its effectiveness in a scientific manner, we do know that some of these herbs work. For instance, the white men discovered the basic ingredient of aspirin when they saw some Indians chewing on the bark of a tree to relieve their pain and fever.

The herb shops in Chinatown can be recognized by rows and rows of small wooden drawers behind the counter. The herbalist fills a prescription from the doctor by taking out small amounts of the contents of the drawers. These are measured very carefully with a little brass scale and poured onto a sheet of clean white paper. The herbs are brewed according to instructions given by the doctor. In some herb shops you will see the figure of a reclining woman carved in ivory. These figures were used by doctors making sick calls on women. In olden times, if a woman had a pain in her shoulder she would point to that spot on the figure. The doctor did not examine her directly.

Acupuncture—the use of needles inserted into key points in the body—is another method used by the Chinese to restore health. Recently, interest in the treatment of illnesses by acupuncture has increased greatly in the United States. Western doctors and newspapermen have reported on its use in hospitals in China. Some people question this practice because it is foreign and strange to them, but acupuncture has been practiced by the Chinese for centuries. Research to determine the principle and effectiveness of acupuncture is now being done in many European and American hospitals.

For close to a hundred years, the Chinatowns in the United States remained small because few Chinese people were permitted to come to this country and none could become a citizen. Under such conditions, there was little opportunity to establish families here. The sick and old went back to China. Many of the younger men returned to their wives and children as soon as they had earned enough money.

The Chinese did not feel part of this country because they were not permitted to become part of it. When the United States changed its policies and its laws, the Chinese felt differently. The men sent for their wives and children. Instead of an all-male community, an increasing number of women and young children began to be seen on Chinatown streets.

In 1965, the Chinese population began to increase rapidly. Chinatowns' boundaries stretched. Sometimes there was no place to push further and housing became an acute problem. The small businesses, shops, and restaurants could not provide jobs for all the newcomers, but the immigrant who could not speak English and was unfamiliar with his new surroundings found it hard to get a job outside his community.

Industries such as the garment, food, and costume jewelry industries moved into Chinatowns to utilize the labor of the immigrant women. When the women left their homes and children to work in the factories, family problems began cropping up.

Once proud of their ability to solve their own problems, Chinatowns are now facing difficulties. The family associations, which were effective in the past in dealing with old problems, can no longer cope with the rapid increase in numbers and the complexity of new problems.

Chinatowns are undergoing a trying period of transition. Behind the glittering neon lights, the exotic scene, the aroma of delectable foods, and the quaintness of an ethnic community, there are people struggling to accommodate themselves to a way of life between East and West.

Chapter Eight

 FAMILY LIFE

A very popular form of greeting among the Chinese used to be "May you have many sons."

Someone who is not familiar with Chinese attitudes might think "What a peculiar thing to say!" But from the Chinese point of view it is just like saying "Good luck" or "Good fortune." In fact, many sons meant more than that.

The Chinese wanted large families because they believed in ancestor worship. Ancestors were honored in death as well as in life and had to be cared for. The names of the departed were placed on tablets on the family altar. On feast days and special occasions, food, paper money, and other offerings were placed before the altar. If the family line died out, the spirits of the family ancestors would go hungry and be ill-clothed for all eternity.

Many sons insured the continuity of the family. To die without a male offspring was a sin of the first order. A man with many sons was counted blessed. A woman without sons had no position or standing.

Daughters were married off when they became of age, so they did not count. Once married, the woman belonged to her husband's family.

For centuries, the family has been the basis of Chinese culture. But family was more than just parents and children. It was a kinship group like a clan. Grown-up sons did not marry and move away. They stayed in the ancestral home, so that a family included many generations—grandparents, uncles, aunts, and cousins as well as parents, brothers, and sisters.

The families were very close-knit. Every man worked for the entire family, not just his own wife and children. If his brother died, he was responsible for the support of his brother's widow and children. The old folks could depend upon their sons for support just as children depend upon their parents to rear them.

In such large families, order and rank were important. Age was the deciding factor. The younger ones had to defer to the older ones. Special terms indicated a person's rank and relationship to another in the family.

In English, the word *uncle* can mean the older brother, younger brother, or husband of the sister of either parent. There is no confusion about relationship or order of birth in the Chinese family. *Bok* is father's older brother. *Soak* is his younger brother. *Kew* is mother's younger brother. *Goo* is father's sister. *Yee* is mother's sister, and so on.

Love and respect for one's parents was the primary virtue. Above all else, children were taught to obey and honor their parents. The children had to respect the wishes of their parents even when they had become adults and had children of their own.

Women were lower in rank than men. A woman had little social position until she had borne a son. Then she was respected as a mother. A woman with many grown sons and grandchildren had a great deal of authority.

In a kinship family, marriage was not a private affair between a man and a woman. It was a family concern. A bride was chosen for the groom by his parents or his elders. A lot of consideration was given to the girl's background and upbringing. Would she fit into the family? Was she strong and healthy so she could bear many sons?

The ancestral home was permanent. No one left it for good. If the men had to go elsewhere to seek their fortunes, they left their wives and children at home. They returned at periodic intervals. Feast days, weddings, funerals, and birthdays were always occasions for homecoming.

That is why when the Chinese set sail for the Mountain of Gold they did not bring their wives and children with them. Only the men came. Then when the exclusion laws were passed, the doors to the United States clanged shut. The men were caught here without any families.

To a people used to a large family circle, this was a very cruel ordeal. Most of the Chinese in this country were grown men with all the responsibilities of son, husband, and father. But they were denied the joys of family life.

The men stayed because it was easier to earn money in America. The region from which most of the Chinese emigrated was over-populated. Farming was the main occupation. Scraping a living from the rocky terrain and depleted soil was very difficult.

With money coming from abroad, the families in China were fairly well off. They may not have had to work in the fields. The children were sent to school. The towns and villages prospered. The sacrifices were made by the husbands and fathers and uncles in the United States, who endured years of lonely separation from their loved ones. Strong bonds bound these families together in spirit, but thousands of miles of ocean and land kept them apart physically.

Occasionally the men made trips back to China. By necessity these were few and far between. The distance was long. The trip was costly. But the greatest deterrents were the harassment of the Chinese at the ports, when they tried to re-enter the country, and the fears that they could not come back in.

The exclusion laws were repealed in 1943 but three more years passed before World War II ended in the Pacific. The men rushed back to China to see their families and, if possible, to bring them to the United States. Those who were citizens could do so. Those who were not had to apply under the 105 quota. The waiting list was a long one.

Many men who had come to the United States as boys had never had the opportunity to marry. Chinese women in this country were few and much sought after. Most of the men had to go to Hong Kong to find brides. Families with eligible daughters fought to get them married to someone from the Mountain of Gold. After the wedding, the wives followed their husbands to the United States. A few special laws passed by the Congress, such as the War Brides Act, made it possible for the wives to come.

Nine out of ten Chinese coming into the country in the years immediately following the end of World War II were women and children. There were few Chinese families in this country until that time.

*Chinese women and children
in ancient traditional dress*

The women brought with them many of the traditions of Chinese family life. However, the clan system was not practical here. The family unit generally consisted of husband, wife, and children. But grandparents were usually part of the elder son's household.

Family ties remained strong. Uncles, aunts, cousins were considered close family members. They had a say in the upbringing of the children.

Members were loyal and helped one another as much as possible. One member's honor reflected upon his whole family. In the same way, one person's disgrace was a shame to the entire family. Parents were held accountable for their children's behavior.

The parents taught their children respect for their elders. They were strict disciplinarians. In a very delightful book, *Fifth Chinese Daughter*, by Jade Snow Wong, the author said, "A little girl never questioned the commands of Mother and Father unless prepared to receive painful consequences."

Pardee Lowe wrote of his mother in his autobiography, *Father and Glorious Descendant*, "She knew only too well how to wield the wrong end of a pliant bamboo duster. With this Rod of Purification, she directed our lives, and we became, as our Chinese friends put it, 'model children who had partaken generously of parental instruction.' "

Harold Lui sums up his childhood experiences with these words: "There was never any question of right or wrong. If my parents disapproved it was wrong."

The people who made these statements were second-generation Chinese-Americans born of parents who came from China. They are now parents of third-generation Chinese-Americans and no longer adhere strictly to the Chinese way of bringing up children.

In all likelihood, the subsequent generations of American-born Chinese will live outside of Chinatown. They are influenced by their American upbringing. They may preserve some of the Chinese customs, but they cannot help but adopt many of the American ways.

When the children refuse to accept the values and customs of a China they do not know and as they pull away from strict parental control, family conflict results.

Most immigrant groups go through this same experience in trying to bridge two cultures. For the Chinese in the United States, who have had little family life until recent years, the process is just beginning.

Chapter Nine

 CHINESE NEW YEAR

Zzzz. . . . Boom! Bang! Boom boom! Bang bang! Firecrackers exploded everywhere.

The noise split the air. It bounced off the tall buildings surrounding Chinatown. The echo added to the volume.

String after string of firecrackers went off in front of stores and homes. An occasional louder boom came from the cherry bombs set off by teen-age boys.

A stooped and gray-haired woman went to the door of her house. In her hands she carried a brown paper bag and long, lighted punk. She reached into the bag, pulled out a small firecracker, lit the fuse with the punk, and threw it into the street. Pop! went the little firecracker. She pulled out another firecracker—and another. Pop! Pop!

Firecrackers are an important part of any Chinese celebration. The noise adds to the gaiety of the festivities and is supposed to scare away the evil spirits.

Down the street, the dragon was prancing and

A Chinese New Year procession in San Francisco

dancing to the clang of cymbals and the beat of drums. The enormous dragon head, held aloft by the lead dancer, was richly decorated with many-colored frills and tassels and bells.

The dragon stopped in front of a store, where the dancers saw a long cord. From it dangled a head of lettuce, a tangerine, a piece of coconut, and money wrapped in red paper.

around the turn of the century

The dragon bowed. He shook his head and with a low swoop went into his routine. The long line of dancers holding the dragon tail twisted and turned, undulating like a snake.

The drums and cymbals beat louder and louder. The noise and din was increased by more strings of firecrackers thrown from the store. They exploded around the feet of the dragon dancers.

The dragon reached for the lettuce on the cord. He tore it to shreds and scattered the leaves. He grabbed the tangerine and the coconut. Next came the money wrapped in red paper. Someone from the store pulled the cord up. The dragon had to stretch higher. He could not reach it.

A dancer from the tail moved in under the dragon head. The head dancer leaped onto the shoulders of the tail dancer, all the time keeping rhythm to the beat of the drums. This time, the elevated dragon reached the packet of money. He snapped the cord, made another bow before the store, and moved on down the street.

This store was now protected by the dragon for the new year. The evil spirits no longer dared lurk.

The occasion was Chinese New Year, and Chinatown was celebrating the first day of the first moon of the lunar calendar. The Chinese base their calendar on the moon, not the sun. That is why New Year's Day does not come on the same date as on the Western calendar. The beginning of the year may fall anywhere between January 20 and February 20.

The beginning of a new moon marks the beginning of a new month. And the fifteenth is always a full moon. That means a month may be twenty-nine or thirty days, so that twelve months is only 354 days. Every two or three years, there's a thirteenth month to make the year and seasons come out right. But the New Year begins on the second new moon after the winter solstice, which is the shortest day of the year.

The years are figured in cycles of twelve, and each is identified by the name of an animal. The twelve animals are the rat, ox, tiger, rabbit, dragon, snake, horse, sheep, monkey, chicken, dog, and pig.

For instance, the year 1970 was the year of the dog. A person who was born that year presumably has some of the characteristics of a dog.

Chinese New Year is the single most important event of the year. For everyone, it not only marks renewed hopes for a better year, it is also everyone's birthday. When the clock strikes midnight on the first day of the first moon, everyone is a year older.

If a baby happened to be born on New Year's Eve,

he is two years old the next day. A baby's age is one the moment he is born. He is two the following New Year's Day.

The Chinese government gave up the lunar calendar and now uses the Western calendar officially. But the people still observe the holidays and festivities according to the lunar calendar.

Chinese New Year's celebrations extend over a month. Weeks before the first day of the first moon, the house is cleaned from top to bottom. The rooms are filled with potted plants and fragrant flowers. The favorites are chrysanthemums, water lilies, red roses, and miniature kumquat trees.

Couplets expressing happy sayings or good wishes are written with a brush on red paper and pasted over the doorways.

In the living room, a table is arranged with tangerines, oranges and pomelos. The word for these citrus fruits has the same sound as the word for good luck, so that they are traditional foods for joyous occasions.

Special treats are pastries and sweets—red melon seeds, sugared coconut strips, preserved fruits, and candies.

Families in China who believe in the deities keep a picture of the kitchen god pasted above the stove. At the end of the year they send their kitchen god to heaven to make his yearly report. He is dispatched there in flames. Before setting fire to his picture it is customary to smear his mouth with sugar to sweeten his report in heaven. After New Year's Day the kitchen god is welcomed home by pasting another picture over the stove.

The last meal of the year is the most elaborate and most significant. It is called *tuan-yuan,* or literally "group around." New Year's Eve is a family festival and everyone stays home instead of going out.

New Year's Day is a day for visiting and feasting. The children pay their respects to their elders and receive gifts of money wrapped in red paper. These are called *hung-bao.* Everyone wishes one another *kung hay fat choy*—best wishes for a happy and prosperous New Year.

Another feast called *hoy nien* starts the New Year. Then families visit back and forth, eating, drinking, talking, playing mah-jongg. Everyone is careful to say and do the right thing, for superstition has it that what happens on New Year's Day determines the events for the coming year.

Certain things are forbidden on the first day of the New Year. These are spanking, crying, sweeping the floor, or washing the hair. If the floor is swept the family luck may be swept away. Loose hair is a sign of mourning. Some families are careful not

to use knives lest the family fortunes be cut in two.

To the Chinese, the New Year is a time to begin a new slate. This means finishing chores left undone, settling disagreements and, most important, paying off all debts by the end of the old year.

In China, the New Year's celebration lasts at least seven days, but generally ends with the Feast of Lanterns on the fifteenth day of the first moon. The parade of colorful and original lanterns brings the holiday season to a close.

In the United States, Chinese-American families do not have time to observe the New Year in such an elaborate fashion. Each family follows those customs that have meaning and memories or sentiments for them. They may just go to Chinatown to watch the fireworks and dragon dance. Or they may eat the traditional foods and visit their families.

The family associations, however, take this occasion to have an annual banquet or get-together. Restaurants in Chinatown are sometimes booked solid through March for these festive events.

Even if Chinese-Americans do not observe any of the other Chinese holidays, they like to celebrate the New Year. It is so full of joy, fun, tradition, and ritual.

A modern-day child in traditional dress visits a shrine during the New Year festivities

Chapter Ten

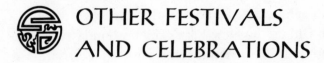 OTHER FESTIVALS
AND CELEBRATIONS

One way to learn about the people of another culture is to see how they observe their festivals and the
important events of their lives.

Aside from Chinese New Year, which is the single
most important annual celebration, there are three
other main folk festivals.

Ch'ing Ming, the Spring Festival, falls on the
third day of the third month of the Chinese calendar. By the Western calendar it is sometime in April.

This is the day families visit and sweep the graves
of their ancestors. To the Chinese who believe in
ancestor worship, this holiday has important religious significance.

It is the duty of each new generation in the family

lineage to take care of those who went before. Sons carry on the family name and an obligation not to break the family line. Their belief is that those in the spiritual world need someone in the earthly sphere to supply their needs.

To those who believe in a divination system called *Feng-shui*, literally "wind and water," the position and condition of the ancestral graves have an important influence on the family fortunes. For instance, a grave facing east instead of southeast may bring illness or calamity upon the family. This is the ancestral spirit's way of calling attention to the fact that his soul is not at peace.

In the United States, these beliefs have given way as more Chinese have become Christians. Burial of the deceased in this country is only a recent happening because, formerly, the Chinese sent their dead back to China. For these reasons the Spring Festival is little observed in this country.

Usually only the men in the family visit the graves. They clear away the debris and weeds. At the gravesite, they pour some wine on the ground. They bow and make an offering of three kinds of meat—pork, chicken, and fish. A sweet, flat, white gelatinous cake is the traditional food for the Spring Festival. Incense and spiritual money are burned.

The important aspect of any religious ritual is its symbolic significance. There is a story about a Chinese and a Caucasian visiting their respective family graves. The Caucasian placed a bouquet of flowers before the grave and stood for a moment in silent meditation. Then he watched the Chinese man go through the motions of offering wine, food, and money.

"Come now," he jested. "Do you really think your ancestors can eat the food, drink the wine, and spend the money?"

"As much as your ancestors can sniff your flowers," replied the Chinese.

The fifth day of the fifth moon is the Dragon Boat Festival. Usually it falls in June, when the weather is warm and balmy.

In China, the day is celebrated with dragon boat races and the eating of sticky rice cakes wrapped and steamed in bamboo leaves.

This festival is celebrated in honor of a prime minister, Chu Yuan, who lived more than two thousand years ago. Chu Yuan was a very capable man who managed to keep his country out of war while neighboring states were continually fighting. His political enemies were jealous of him and accused him of wrongdoing. He was banished by the emperor to a faraway place.

Chu Yuan was very sad. He wrote a poem called "Parting Sorrow," which told of his love for his country and how he wanted peace for his people.

Then he threw himself into the river on the fifth day of the fifth moon.

When the people read his poem, they realized how deeply he loved his country and how he had been wronged. His spirit reappeared and asked that rice cakes be dropped into the river for him. Fishermen rowed out to the middle of the river to drop the rice cakes. In time, the custom of boat races developed.

In the United States, the Chinese eat the sticky rice cakes to mark the festival. Some of the rice cakes are sweet. Most are stuffed with meat, sausages, egg yolks, soy beans, or peanuts. They are wrapped in large bamboo leaves and steamed in huge kettles for more than five hours.

Instead of dragon boat races, Chinatown organizations charter excursion boats for an outing on the waters.

The Mid-Autumn Festival falls on the fifteenth day of the eighth moon. The festival, celebrated at night, is mainly for the women and girls. When the full moon lights up the darkness of the skies, all the females of a household gather in the courtyard or sit by open windows with their offerings to the moon. These include thick round moon cakes filled with melon seeds, lotus seeds, or crushed black soy beans.

Grapes, pomegranates, and peaches are also offered. These seed foods symbolize fertility. The peach symbolizes long life.

All over the world, the moon is associated with romance. The Mid-Autumn Festival is the night for secret rites when the girls try to find out what their future husbands are like. The girls strum on their musical instruments and chant their songs of love under the silvery rays of the moon.

The Mid-Autumn Festival is also a harvest festival and a day of thanksgiving. It comes at a time when the crops are in and the gods are to be thanked for their bounties.

Among Chinese-American families, the day is generally observed by eating the traditional moon cakes and fruits and gazing at the moon. The moon always seems rounder and larger on the night of the Mid-Autumn Festival.

A day that used to be celebrated with a great deal of fanfare among the Chinese in the United States was Double-Ten. The two tens stood for the tenth day of October according to the Western calendar.

The day commemorated the overthrow of the Manchu Dynasty by Dr. Sun Yat-sen and the establishment of a republican form of government in China. Political speeches and a parade generally marked the day in Chinatown.

Double-Ten has lost much of its significance. The day is associated with a government no longer in power in China. October 1 is now the national holi-

The people of New York's Chinatown used to celebrate October 10 with lively parades

day in China. It commemorates the inauguration in 1949 of the Central People's Government of the Chinese People's Republic.

Birth, marriage, and death are the three great events in life. In every country and with every people, these occasions are surrounded with ceremonies and customs. In China, there are elaborate rituals for marking these events, but in the United States they are modified and simplified to suit the circumstances.

A new baby is always a joyous event, for the Chinese prize large families. Right after the birth, two foods are given the mother to help her regain her strength—pig's feet cooked in vinegar and chicken cooked in rice wine. Visitors who come to congratulate the parents are also offered these foods.

The baby's arrival is announced by giving out eggs dipped in a red dye. Two eggs announce a boy; one, a girl. The phrase "eating red eggs" means the same as welcoming a new baby.

If the baby is a boy, there is usually a banquet for the close relatives. The banquet takes place a month after the birth and is called the "shaving-the-head" feast. At that time, a tiny lock is shaved from the infant's head.

It is not necessary to have a banquet for a girl baby unless the parents are very well-to-do. As the families get larger, the banquets are even omitted for the younger sons.

The most elaborate celebrations are reserved for weddings. The younger generations and more modern Chinese like to follow the Western customs. They are married in a Christian church. The bride wears the traditional long white gown and veil.

Most Chinese-American weddings retain some of the Chinese customs. The wedding invitation may be on red paper engraved in gold lettering. Chinese writing is printed on the left, English on the right.

The groom's family may send the bride hundreds of moon cakes like the ones eaten during the Mid-Autumn Festival. These are given out and serve as announcements to the bride's friends and relatives, who send her wedding gifts.

It is customary for the bride's family to give the young couple furniture, household goods, and money as a dowry.

After the church ceremony, the young couple may go through the ritual of paying their respects to the elders and members of the groom's family. The bride and groom bow before the groom's parents. With both hands, the groom offers his parents a betel nut, and the bride offers her new in-laws small cups of tea. In turn, the parents give their son a *hung-bao*, the packet of good luck money wrapped in red paper. The daughter-in-law usually receives gifts of jade and gold jewelry.

Betel nuts and tea are proffered to other close relatives and elders on the groom's side. Everyone gives the bride and groom *hung-bao*.

The groom's family gives the wedding banquet. The eating and drinking go on for hours as twelve or more courses are served. Before one dish is emptied, another is brought out.

For the wedding banquet, the bride changes to a red or pink satin dress embroidered with flowers or sequins. Red is the color for weddings.

Throughout the banquet, the men drink wine and play finger games. Two men play at a time. Each puts out a number of fingers and shouts a number at the same time. If the number he shouts equals the number of fingers extended by both men together, he wins. The loser has to drink up. The object is to get the other man drunk.

The groom goes to each of the tables urging his guests to eat and drink. Then the bride, accompanied by her bridesmaids, visits every table and offers each guest a tiny cup of tea. The guests sip the tea and return the cup to the bride with a red envelope of good luck money.

Certain rituals are associated with funerals. White is the color of mourning in China but the Chinese in this country usually follow the Western funeral customs. Then the mourning color is black. However, the Chinese keep many of the old traditions. Instead of flower wreaths, friends and relatives may send long lengths of materials called blankets, which are draped over the coffin of the deceased. They also send money in white envelopes.

Friends and relatives come to pay their last respects. Usually a picture of the deceased is placed at the head of the coffin. Two candles at the foot serve to light the way to the afterworld.

If the funeral service is not a Christian one, Buddhist monks may chant their sutras and burn incense and *gee-bao*. This is afterworld money so that the deceased may be provided for in the hereafter. Sometimes paper clothes, paper furniture, a paper house, and other items are burned and sent to the deceased spirit in this way.

After the funeral rites, each guest is given a coin and a piece of candy to sweeten the bitterness of his grief. A lavish meal is served to close friends and relatives after their return from the burial.

When the deceased has lived a long and useful life and has many sons and daughters and grandchildren, the funeral loses some of its somber air. It becomes an occasion for a family reunion and provides an opportunity to recount the blessings of the deceased during his lifetime.

In observing these rites and rituals, Chinese-Americans keep alive the traditions of their ancient culture. But more and more American holidays like Easter, the Fourth of July, Thanksgiving, and Christmas are taking precedence over the Chinese festivals. Before long, the rich heritage of Chinese folklore may be lost altogether.

Chapter Eleven

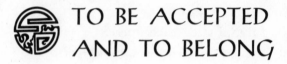 ## TO BE ACCEPTED AND TO BELONG

The Chinese were never really a part of America until after World War II. The small number of Chinese who lived here kept their ways and kept to themselves. The larger American society refused to let any more Chinese come in, and life was made very difficult for the ones who were here.

For example, the Second Constitution of California of 1879 forbade corporations to hire Chinese, denied Chinese the right to vote, forbade them employment on public works, annulled all contracts for "coolie labor," and imposed restrictions on where the Chinese could live.

These restrictions were written into the supreme

law of California in complete disregard for human rights, for international obligations, and in spite of guarantees under the United States Constitution.

In 1906, San Francisco decided that Oriental children could not attend white schools. Shortly thereafter, the states of Washington, Oregon, and California passed Alien Land Acts forbidding Orientals to own land.

In 1928, the Stanford University Placement service said, "It is impossible to place a Chinese or Japanese of either the first or second generation in any kind of position, engineering, manufacturing, or business."

Fifteen states made it a crime for a white person to marry an Oriental. The Chinese could not testify in court. They could not apply for naturalization. Other laws imposed special taxes against them. Discrimination had the backing of laws!

Under similar circumstances, some oppressed people fight back. Some submit. The Chinese chose to withdraw. They simply kept to themselves, maintained their own customs and institutions, stayed in Chinatowns, and looked to the day when they could go back to China.

It was a form of accommodation. As their numbers shrank, the American people gradually forgot about the Chinese. Their intense animosity faded away.

In 1937 Japan attacked China, starting a global war that was to last until 1946. By 1949 the Communists had taken over the mainland. The Chinese in the United States found their goal blocked. They could no longer go back to China. Besides, they wanted to stay.

Fortunately, the American attitude toward the Chinese had changed for the better. The United States and China had been allies in arms. Shortage of labor during the war forced some companies to hire Chinese. Once they were hired, a lot of false ideas about the Chinese vanished. When they proved that they could do their jobs and do them well, the barriers of prejudice began to topple.

In 1940 only 3 per cent of the Chinese were in professions like medicine, teaching, science, and engineering. By 1960 this percentage had jumped sixfold to 18 per cent. This proportion is even higher than for white Americans.

What enabled the Chinese to get ahead so quickly? In large measure, the answer lies in the Chinese respect for learning. The professions require many years of education and training. Even when the Chinese knew that they could not get good jobs here, they still tried to get as good an education as possible. They figured they could always use their skills and knowledge in China. The Chinese were ready and qualified for the positions they sought when the walls of discrimination were lowered.

Some companies even seek out Chinese, who have established for themselves a reputation for hard work and reliability. Nevertheless, the Chinese look upon their achievement with some measure of reserve. They have not forgotten that they were once praised and welcomed before.

The last publicized case of housing discrimination against a Chinese occurred in 1952. Sheng Sing

Occupations of the Chinese in the United States

1960

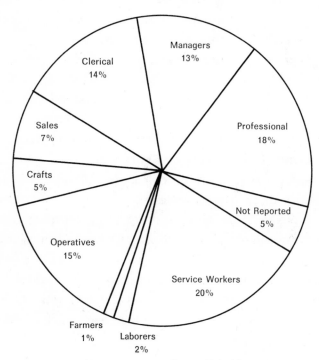

Source: United States Census.

bought a home in Southwood, California, a little town of four hundred families. Some of the neighbors learned that a Chinese family was moving in. They protested.

Sheng Sing believed in the democratic process. He offered to put the issue to a vote. When the vote was counted, Sheng Sing was stunned. Out of 202 votes, 174 votes were against him.

When news of this incident leaked out, the public was furious. Newspapers, church leaders, decent citizens everywhere condemned the vote. Within two days, Sheng Sing received thirty offers to sell him a home in other suburban sections of San Francisco where he would be welcomed.

Two weeks after the Sheng Sing incident, Freddie Wing bought a home in Sonoma, California, not far from Southwood. Freddie was very uneasy. He had read about the Sheng Sing case. Nevertheless, he made plans for his housewarming. As if to make up for the bad manners of Southwood, the neighborhood turned out in force to give Freddie and his family an uproarious welcome.

In New York City, another large center of Chinese population, no case of discrimination against Chinese in housing has ever been reported to the City Commission on Human Rights. This does not mean that there has been no discrimination whatsoever. It may be that the Chinese never make an issue of it.

*A group of
teen-agers from
New York's
Chinatown*

The Chinese in the United States get along very
well with their fellow Americans. They are respected—and were respected even when they were
being persecuted—for their strong moral qualities,
for their hard work, for their honor, and for their
low crime rate. Expensive cars, houses, furs, and the
like are not the Chinese-Americans' symbols of social
success. In their scale of values, scholarship, position,
and family come first.

The discriminatory laws mentioned at the beginning of this chapter have long ago been thrown out by the courts or repealed. Those on intermarriage lasted the longest. They were finally struck down by a Supreme Court decision in 1967.

Surprisingly, the rate of marriage between the Chinese and other races is very high—about one out of every four. If this rate continues, even the physical identity of the Chinese will soon be blurred.

In 1900, one out of ten Chinese was American-born. By 1960, six out of ten were born in this country. As the number of native-born increases, the group will become more Americanized.

The Chinese population in the United States is no longer homogeneous—in other words, one and alike. There are old-timers. These are the ones who remain in their traditional occupations and cling to the old ways.

There are newcomers. Some are highly skilled and educated. They are searching for a new life in this country. Their Chinese upbringing is deeply ingrained. But they are not handicapped by the scars of anti-Chinese prejudice. They and their children are looking for a place in American society.

The native-born are Americans, but their physical features mark them as Chinese. This is a dual identity which they must integrate, drawing upon both their Chinese heritage and their American birthright.

Chapter Twelve

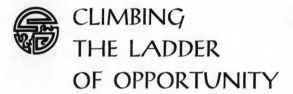 CLIMBING
THE LADDER
OF OPPORTUNITY

The Chinese can trace their history in the United States back for more than 120 years. The first hundred were marked by hardship, struggle, and rejection. Only within the last twenty years have they been offered the opportunity to become a part of America and to advance themselves. Yet within this short span of time the Chinese have made remarkable progress. Their contributions to this country and to all mankind have been enormous and far-reaching.

A few have gained world fame in such varied fields as government, science, business, and the arts. Their stories are told in the following pages.

*Senator Hiram Fong
was a favorite-son
nominee for president
at the Republican
National Convention
in San Francisco in 1964*

UNITED STATES SENATOR HIRAM FONG

Senator Hiram Fong was voted into one of the highest elective offices in the land in 1959. His personal popularity was so great that he was elected as a Republican from a Democratic state. He is the first

American of Asian descent to be elected to the Senate. And he was that state's first member in Congress after Hawaii was admitted to the Union.

In 1964 and again in 1968 he was a favorite-son nominee for Republican candidate for President of the United States. In 1970, he was re-elected to the Senate for a third six-year term.

Senator Fong's rise from the slums of Kaliki is a good example of the American success story. His parents had come from China to work on the sugar plantations. Born in 1907, Hiram was the seventh of eleven children.

With so many mouths to feed, every member of the Fong family had to do his share. With his brothers and sisters, Hiram was picking mesquite beans for cattle feed when he was only four years old.

By the time he was seven, Hiram was shining shoes, selling newspapers, catching and selling fish and crabs, delivering *poi*, and caddying, even when the golf bags were bigger than he.

The family was poor. The parents were field workers who could not read or write. But they insisted that all eleven of their children get as much schooling as possible. To go through high school for free! Perhaps even to the university! That was undreamed-of in China.

Even if the schools charged no tuition, it was not easy for children of the poor to get an education.

The Fong children had to work at jobs as well as go to school. Hiram's parents needed his wages to help keep food on the table. It was three years after graduation from high school before Hiram could afford to go to college.

Time was precious to Hiram. He decided to finish college in three years instead of four. Then he set his sights on Harvard Law School. He did not know how he was going to get there, but his goal was firmly fixed. Five years later, he returned to Honolulu from Harvard with his hard-earned law degree, ten cents in his pocket, and a pile of debts.

Today, Senator Fong's law practice and business investments have made him a millionaire. In his business, he applied the same principles as he did to his studies—ingenuity and hard work.

In 1938, three years after he had graduated from law school, Hiram Fong was elected to the Hawaii Legislature. Six years later he had risen to become Vice-Speaker of the House of Representatives. Another two terms and he was in the number one spot as Speaker of the House.

At that time, Hawaii was not a state. It was only a territory. Hiram Fong worked very hard to bring Hawaii into the Union as the fiftieth state. This dream was realized in 1959. For his long years of service and devotion to Hawaii, the people sent him to Congress as their first senator.

PHYSICISTS CHEN NING YANG, TSUNG DAO LEE, AND CHIEN SHIUNG WU

Three of the most famous physicists in the world today are Chinese-Americans. They are Drs. Chen Ning Yang, Tsung Dao Lee, and Chien Shiung Wu.

Drs. Yang and Lee jointly won the Nobel Prize for physics in 1957. Dr. Wu is considered one of the world's foremost experimental physicists.

Working together, the three shattered a universally accepted physical "law"—the principle of the conservation of parity.

On January 15, 1957, the *New York Times* described this discovery as "the most important development in physics in the past ten years." It went on to say:

> This discovery, by removing the major roadblock that stood in the way of understanding the meaning of the newest particles in the atomic nucleus, promises at last to clear a straight road into the open out of the present atomic "jungle." It may be likened to the final realization that the earth was not flat, which opened the way to the understanding of the motions of planets, the stars and the galaxies and to the laws of motion in general, which led directly to the Machine Age, as well as to the age of electricity, radio, television and earth satellites. The fruits of the new discovery

Dr. Chien Shiung Wu is considered one of the world's foremost experimental physicists

may not ripen for another quarter century or more, but scientists are now confident that they are at last on the right road to a better understanding of the forces that govern our universe, and very likely to their utilization for the benefit of all mankind.

At the time of this important discovery, Dr. Yang was a member of the Institute for Advanced Study at Princeton. He was thirty-four years old. Dr. Lee was a professor of physics at Columbia University. He was thirty years old and the youngest full professor on the faculty.

To prove their discovery, Professors Yang and Lee turned to Dr. Chien Shiung Wu to conduct the difficult experiments that Drs. Lee and Yang suggested. She is also a professor of physics at Columbia University.

Within six months, Dr. Wu finished her experiments. She announced to a startled world that a physical "law" of nature had been disproved. Insurmountable obstacles, based on application of this "law," were now removed. Physicists think that the new findings may lead to a new concept of order and harmony in the universe.

Professors Lee, Yang, and Wu graduated from colleges in China. They came to the United States for their higher education. Originally they intended to go back to China when their studies were completed. War and the political situation in China made them change their minds.

In this country their genius was quickly recognized. They were given a chance to work closely with eminent scientists like J. Robert Oppenheimer and Enrico Fermi.

Just as these men sparked the minds of Drs. Chen Ning Yang, Tsung Dao Lee, and Chien Shiung Wu, they, in turn, are nurturing the future scientists of America.

Dr. Yang is now Distinguished Professor of Physics at Stony Brook University on Long Island, New York. He occupies the Albert Einstein Chair of Science. His presence at Stony Brook has attracted some of the foremost scientists and scholars to this branch of the State University of New York and has placed it in the forefront of modern physics.

BIOCHEMIST CHOH HAO LI

Dr. Choh Hao Li may be another Nobel Prize winner. His field is biochemistry and medicine.

In 1962 he was named winner of the Albert Lasker Medical Research Award. This is one of the highest awards for basic medical research in the United States. Many of its recipients have gone on to receive the Nobel Prize.

Dr. Li is considered the world's foremost authority on the pituitary gland. This gland lies at the base of the brain. It is called the master gland because it regulates the growth and function of the other glands in the body.

From the secretions of the pituitary gland, Dr. Li isolated ACTH, HGH, and four other hormones.

People who suffer painful joints from rheumatoid arthritis and rheumatic fever are very grateful to Dr. Li for ACTH. The drug has been used successfully for the treatment of these diseases. Children whose growth is stunted by a lack of HGH are helped to grow to a normal size with injections of HGH.

It used to take 5,000 human pituitaries taken from autopsies to yield a sixth of an ounce of the hormones. Dr. Li had to find a way to make these hormones in the laboratory. Five years of research followed his discovery of ACTH before he learned how to duplicate nature. Ten more years of work fol-

Dr. Choh Hao Li has made remarkable contributions to the field of biochemistry

lowed before he was successful with HGH. For his discoveries, Dr. Li has been honored by many organizations and foreign governments.

Dr. Li was born in Canton, China. He came to this country in 1935 as a student. He studied at the University of California under a great teacher, Dr. Herbert McClean Evans, who pioneered in the study of the pituitary gland. Dr. Li followed in his teacher's footsteps. He has spent a lifetime studying this tiny organ at the same university, where he is now director of the Hormone Research Laboratory.

FINANCIER GERALD TSAI, JR.

The world of high finance is practically closed to members of dark-skinned minority groups. But in 1966, a young Chinese-American by the name of Gerald Tsai, Jr., scaled the walls.

On the strength of his name and reputation alone, a hundred and fifty thousand investors entrusted him with $270 million to start the Manhattan Fund. A record was set when $19 million worth of shares was sold in a single day. Wall Street regulars—accustomed as they were to large sums—were absolutely flabbergasted.

Gerald Tsai (pronounced sigh) came to the United States when he was eighteen years old. He became an American citizen in 1957. Tsai graduated from Boston University. Then he went to work for Bache & Co. at fifty dollars a week.

Gerald did not stay long at that level. He left Bache to run the Fidelity Fund of Boston. Fourteen years later, Mr. Harold Bache himself handed Gerald Tsai a check for $247,050,000 as underwriter for the Manhattan Fund. Mr. Bache is quite used to writing checks for large sums of money, but he confessed that this was the largest check he had ever written.

As founder and president of the Manhattan Fund, Gerald Tsai manages the money by investing it in stocks and bonds. The hopes of the people who buy his mutual fund shares are that he will invest wisely and increase the value of their shares.

Because he has done so well in the past, other money managers watch him very closely to see what he does. Huge corporations that need large sums of capital confer with Tsai. They know that he has the ability to move large blocks of stock.

For an immigrant who came here in 1946, Gerald Tsai has done well and gone far.

HOLLYWOOD CAMERAMAN
JAMES WONG HOWE

James Wong Howe is a Hollywood cameraman. He is not a star, but on any movie he shoots, he gets star billing. His name goes up in neon lights on the theater marquee right next to the names of the stars of the films.

Newsweek of January 11, 1960, said, "Among movie cameramen, none ranks higher than Jimmy Howe, a Chinese-American veteran of 42 years. Hollywood film director, John Sturges, states flatly, 'He is the greatest stylist in the business.' "

Aaron Sussman, author of photography books, wrote: "Watch especially for those [films] photographed by that amazing Chinese genius, James

Wong Howe. He has made motion picture photography a great art."

James was born near Canton sometime near the turn of the century. The family came to the United States and settled in Pasco, Washington. His father operated two restaurants, a grocery store, and a hardware store.

Young Jimmy wanted to be a prize fighter, but as he was less than five feet tall, he soon gave up that idea.

Wandering around the Plaza of Los Angeles one day, Jimmy came upon the filming of a movie. He was so fascinated that he pestered the studio until they gave him a job. He was paid ten dollars a week to work twelve hours a day moving cameras from place to place. At least he had gotten a toe in the door.

He bought himself an old camera and began experimenting with lights and lenses. One day he asked Mary Minter, then a famous actress, if she would pose for him. She agreed. When she saw the prints she was astounded. They were so magnificent that she demanded that Howe be made her cameraman.

Jimmy said, "Because I was Chinese, people expected me to stay in the background and accept a certain number of insults. I was given the worst equipment on the lot." But Jimmy was used to being picked on. He knew also that to make up for race prejudice he had to be better than the others. When the producers saw what he could do with the wreck of a camera they gave him, they quickly signed him to a contract.

There are a number of "Oscars" on Jimmy's mantel. Movie stars fight over him. One even tried to kidnap him for her film, when she found out that he was signed up to do another at the same time.

In a profession that is creatively demanding and competitive, Jimmy Wong Howe has been at the top for nearly half a century.

ARTIST DONG KINGMAN

"Young man," said the lady peering over the artist's shoulder, "you paint very well. You should exhibit your paintings."

"Thank you, Ma'am." The slight, black-haired man seated on a stool in front of his easel near the Manhattan Bridge grinned.

The lady did not know that Dong Kingman's paintings were already hanging in the permanent collections of more than forty museums and art galleries in the United States. These include the Metropolitan Museum of Art, the Whitney Museum of Modern Art, the Museum of Fine Arts in Boston, the Art Institute of Chicago, and others too numerous to list.

Dong Kingman is recognized as one of America's leading artists. In the medium of water color, he is the leading master.

Dong Kingman was born in California in 1911, the second of eight children. His father ran a laundry. When Dong was five years old, the family decided to go back to Hong Kong. There Dong studied painting by copying the old masters.

His teacher was not strictly of the Chinese school. He had studied in Paris, and he taught young Dong many of the Western approaches to art.

In 1929, at the beginning of the Depression, Dong returned to the land of his birth. He was eighteen years old and on his own. He worked at all sorts of odd jobs, but he wanted to paint. During the Depression, however, artists weren't very much in demand. The hunger pangs were very strong, and Dong had to eat.

Fortunately the Work Projects Administration gave him a chance to paint and eat. The WPA was a program sponsored by the government during the Depression to provide jobs for the needy on worthy public projects.

Dong's very first exhibit in 1933 was a great success. He has not worried about being hungry since. He paints an average of fifty pictures a year. Every one has been sold including a few that have not been painted yet.

In 1954, the United States State Department asked Kingman to represent this country as a cultural envoy to the Orient. His trip was so successful in the Far East that his tour was expanded to take him around the world. Everywhere he went he was received with acclaim and affection. And he established for himself an international reputation.

ARCHITECT IEOH MING PEI

Perched on top of 385 Madison Avenue is a circular penthouse which has become an architectural landmark in New York City. Everything in the penthouse is round—the walls, the elevators, even the furniture.

The penthouse was designed by I. M. Pei.

Downtown and farther east is another of Pei's architectural creations—Kips Bay Plaza. This is an elegant and expensive housing development covering many square blocks.

But Ieoh Ming Pei does not design only luxury apartments. He has been involved in urban renewal and slum clearance projects in almost every major city in the United States.

Mr. Pei's greatest talent as an architect has been

his ability to relate city surroundings to human needs. For example, in the Bedford-Stuyvesant section of Brooklyn, New York, one of the worst slum districts in the city, Mr. Pei works directly with the people of the community. He does not want to move everyone out, level the area to the ground, and put up modern, sterile apartment houses. The community would be lifeless and without character.

By avoiding as much wrecking as possible and making over present streets and buildings, Pei hopes to preserve the charm of the neighborhoods.

In 1968, Columbia University turned to Pei for a long-range plan of expansion.

The planning of a world-famous university campus is more than design and stone and mortar. The product of a great university is the future leaders of the world. The place where they shape their ideas and thoughts must provide for and inspire them to this task.

Columbia University borders on Harlem. The University needs room to grow. Harlem, however, wants to safeguard its boundaries. The problem is how to satisfy the needs and demands of both groups.

In a situation like this, Mr. Pei needs a crystal ball to help him look into the future, and the wisdom of Solomon to help him meet the needs of both sides.

A triumph in Mr. Pei's career came when he was chosen from among eighteen internationally famous architects to design the John F. Kennedy Memorial Library in Boston. When it is finished, millions of people from all over the world will come to see it. Mr. Pei does not intend for it to be an awe-inspiring structure. It will be a living memorial—a national shrine—to the memory of one of America's most beloved presidents.

These are brief chapters in the stories of a few Chinese-Americans who have distinguished themselves. The list is not exhausted. There are many more—Lin Yutang, author; Dr. M. C. Chang, codiscoverer of The Pill; Sze Yi-Kwei, opera singer; Chinn Ho, real estate developer; Dr. M. C. Li, cancer researcher, and so on.

Over 1,500 distinguished Chinese scholars are teaching in colleges and universities. About a hundred Chinese are on the faculties of Harvard, Princeton, and Yale. Many thousands more are teaching in elementary and high schools.

In medicine, in technology, in science, and in the arts, the Chinese are making notable contributions. The future promises higher peaks from the younger generations coming up.

One spring day in 1968, Joseph Alsop, noted journalist, columnist, and political analyst drove through the East Gate of the White House. He was to attend a public reception for Presidential Scholars. These are some of the brightest young high school graduates in the nation—one boy and one girl from each state—who are singled out each year for a Bronze Medal Award for outstanding scholastic achievement.

Mr. Alsop was handed a news release listing the names of the winners. He immediately picked out a glaring fact. Among the hundred names listed, four were of Chinese extraction.

Considering the small number of Chinese in the United States, this proportion of Chinese among the Presidential Scholars for that year was quite impressive to the veteran newsman.

These young students represented the future Chinese-Americans—full of promise and full of hope.

FOR FURTHER READING

Chu, Daniel, and Samuel Chu. *Passage to the Golden Gate*. Garden City, New York: Doubleday & Co., 1967.

Current Biography. An annual magazine.
Hiram Fong (1960 Volume)
James Wong Howe (1943 Volume)
Dong Kingman (1962 Volume)
Choh Hao Li (1963 Volume)
C. N. Yang and T. D. Li (1958 Volume)

Lin Yutang. *Chinatown Family*. New York: John Day & Co., 1948.

Lowe, Pardee. *Father and Glorious Descendant*. Boston: Little Brown & Co., 1943.

Murray, Marian. *Plant Wizard: The Life of Lue Gim Gong*. New York: Crowell-Collier Press, 1970.

Sung, Betty Lee. *Mountain of Gold*. New York: The Macmillan Co., 1967.

Wong, Jade Snow. *Fifth Chinese Daughter*. New York: Harper Bros., 1950.

INDEX